BELLY ACHERS

Over **600** clean, never mean, good for your bean, funniest jokes you've ever seen!

From the Laugh Factory

APPLESAUCE PRESS

13-Digit ISBN: 978-1-60433-276-6
10-Digit ISBN: 1-60433-276-X

This book may be ordered by mail from the publisher. Please include $2.95 for postage and handling. Please support your local bookseller first!

Books published by Cider Mill Press Book Publishers are available at special discounts for bulk purchases in the United States by corporations, institutions, and other organizations. For more information, please contact the publisher.

Applesauce Press is an imprint of
Cider Mill Press Book Publishers
"Where good books are ready for press"
12 Port Farm Road
Kennebunkport, Maine 04046

Visit us on the Web!
www.cidermillpress.com

Design by Tilly Grassa - TGCreative Services
All illustrations courtesy of Anthony Owsley

1 2 3 4 5 6 7 8 9 0
First Edition

CONTENTS

CHAPTER
1
Smart Alecks

Teacher: Richard, find North America on the wall map.

Richard: There it is.

Teacher: Correct. Now class, who discovered North America.

Class: Richard!

* * * * * * * * * * * * * *

Principal: **Don't you enjoy going to school?**

Debbie: **Of course I enjoy going to school. It's the being there that bugs me!**

* * * * * * * * * * * * * *

Teacher: What do you want to get out of high school?

Student: I just want to get out.

* * * * * * * * * * * * * * * * * * *

Teacher: How would you find the square root of 144?

Student: I'd ask the kid sitting next to me.

Teacher: Robert, did you miss school yesterday?

Robert: No way! I didn't miss it one bit.

* * * * * * * * * * * * * *

TEACHER: WHY AREN'T YOU USING YOUR PENCIL TO TAKE THE EXAM?

STUDENT: IT'S POINTLESS.

* *

Teacher: What are you laughing at, Henry?

Henry: Sorry, teacher. I was just thinking of something funny.

Teacher: From now on when you're in my class, don't think.

Teacher: How would you feed twenty people with ten apples?

Girl: Make applesauce.

Principal: Why don't you ever take any books home?

Boy: Because they're school books not home books.

****

TEACHER: WHAT CAN YOU TELL ME ABOUT THE ENGLISH CHANNEL?

BOY: NOTHING. WE DON'T HAVE SATELLITE TV.

Principal: Do you come to school just to make trouble?

Bully: No. I also like recess, lunch, and gym.

Teacher: Do you know what the word extinct means?

Student: It means a skunk died.

Bob: What are you going to do during your summer vacation?
Rob: I'm going to review everything I learned in school the past year.
Bob: And what are you going to do on the second day of vacation?

• •

Teacher: Take a seat. Rupert.
Rupert: Where do you want me to take it, teacher?

• • • • • • • • • • •

Teacher: Why is your report on milk so short?
Girl: I wrote it on condensed milk.

• •

Principal: Why are you always a perfect jokester?
Student: Everyone is good at something, and I also practice a lot.

GIRL: LET'S PLAY SCHOOL. I'LL BE THE TEACHER.

BOY: OKAY. I'LL BE ABSENT.

• •

Mom: Why is your report card soaking wet?
Son: Because all of my grades are below C-level.

• •

Teacher: James! I'm happy to see that you've finally raised your hand.
James: Thank you teacher. Now, can I go to the bathroom?

• •

Father: Gah! You flunked every class.
Boy: Well, I might not be smart, but at least I'm consistent.

• •

Teacher: Does anyone know the name of the First Lady?
Girl: Eve.

Teacher: How long did Thomas Edison live?
Boy: He lived until he died.

Mom: Summer vacation is not the time to stop learning.
Son: Right. I did that the week before school ended.

Principal: You were late every day this week.
Student: That's not true. I was only late four times. The other day I played hooky.

Girl: Why don't you like history class?
Boy: It's always the same old story.

INSTRUCTOR: WHAT'S THE MOST COMMON CAUSE OF DRY SKIN?
MEDICAL STUDENT: TOWELS.

Teacher: Neatness counts on the test you just took, class.
Maggie: In that case, I should get a good grade. My paper doesn't have a mark on it.

Father: Why do you hate the first day of school so much?
Son: Because it's followed by the second day of school and the third day and on and on.

Mother: Why are your grades so low after Christmas vacation?
Girl: You know how it is, Mom. Everything gets marked down after the holidays.

Teacher: What do you know about the Grand Canyon?
Student: It's America's greatest depression.

Teacher: *How did you like our lesson about the Pacific Ocean?*
Student: *All of the facts are just starting to sink in.*

Father: How did you find school today?
Son: It was easy. The bus dropped us off at the main entrance.

Teacher: Zeke, name six wild animals that live in Africa.
Zeke: Three lions, two zebras, and a giraffe.

Teacher: What comes before March?
Military Student: Forward.

MUSIC STUDENT: WHAT ARE THOSE PAPERS THE ORCHESTRA LEADER IS LOOKING AT?

MUSIC TEACHER: THAT'S THE SCORE.

MUSIC STUDENT: OH. WHO WON?

• •

Girl: I know English good.

Boy: I know English "well."

Girl: Then I guess we'll both do good on the exam.

• •

Girl: That's Mr. Smith. He wants to be a member of the school board.

Boy: I'm already a member.

Girl: What do you mean?

Boy: I'm bored with school.

• •

Mother: What did you learn in school today?

Son: Not much. They expect me to go back for more tomorrow.

Teacher: Class! If you don't stop making all this racket, I'll go crazy.
Student: Too late, Teach. We quieted down ten minutes ago.

****

Teacher: What did you write your research paper on?
Student: On my laptop.

****

Teacher: Do you know what procrastination is?

Student: Ask me again later.

Bob: I didn't know anything until I started school.
Rob: Neither did I. And I still don't. But now they test me on it.

TEACHER: WOULD YOU LIKE TO DO SOME ADDITION FOR ME?
STUDENT: I DON'T HAVE A PROBLEM WITH THAT.

Mother: How do you like doing homework?
Daughter: I like doing nothing better.

**Teacher: Why did you stop
referring to that dictionary?
Student: Words no longer have any
meaning for me.**

Teacher: What do you expect to be
when you get out of high school?
Student: Retired.

Teacher: What's
a polygon?
Student: Something
that eventually
turns into a frog.

Teacher: How long does it take you
to do your homework?
Student: About two hours ... three
if Dad helps me.

Teacher: Why are you crawling into my classroom?
Student: Because you said anyone who walks in late gets detention.

▲▲▲▲▲▲▲▲▲▲▲▲▲▲▲▲▲▲▲▲▲▲▲▲▲▲▲▲

STUDENT: I DON'T THINK I DESERVED A ZERO ON THIS EXAM.
TEACHER: I AGREE, BUT IT'S THE LOWEST MARK I CAN GIVE YOU.

▼▼▼▼▼▼▼▼▼▼▼▼▼▼▼▼▼▼▼▼▼▼▼▼▼▼▼▼

Teacher: What's the difference between one yard and two yards?
Marty: A picket fence.

Robert: Teacher, would you punish me for something I didn't do?
Teacher: Or course not.
Robert: That's good, because I didn't do my homework.

Student: **Why did you bring birdseed to school?**
Teacher: **I have a parrot-teacher conference after class.**

Chemistry Teacher: **What do you know about nitrates?**
Student: **Sometimes they're cheaper than day rates.**

Father: I want you to have all of the things I didn't have as a boy.
Son: You mean like "A's" on my report card?

▲▲▲▲▲▲▲▲▲▲▲▲▲▲▲▲▲▲▲▲▲▲▲▲▲▲▲▲▲▲

Teacher: **What will you do when you're as big as your father?**
Boy: **Diet.**

Lunch Lady: Why do you have a pickle behind your ear?
Dork Student: Oh no! I must have eaten my pencil!

. . . .

Teacher: *A noun is a person, place, or thing.*
Student: *Well, make up your mind. Which is it?*

. . . .

Teacher: Did you know Henry Hudson discovered the Hudson River?

Student: Wow! What a coincidence.

. . . .

Teacher: **How many feet are there in a yard?**
Boy: **It depends on how many people are standing in the yard.**

Teacher: Billy Smith, all of the other students in class forgot to do their homework. Did you forget, too?
Billy: No teacher. But tomorrow I'll try harder.

• •

TEACHER: DID YOUR FATHER WRITE THIS COMPOSITION FOR YOU, MARTY?
MARTY: NO TEACHER. HE STARTED IT, BUT MY MOM HAD TO WRITE THE WHOLE THING OVER.

• • • • • • • • • • • • • • • • • •

Teacher: Who was Homer?
Boy: The person Babe Ruth made famous.

Teacher: Can you tell me how fast light travels?
Boy: I don't know, but it always gets here too early in the morning.

Boy: I know the capital of North Carolina.
Teacher: Oh, really?
Boy: No. Raleigh.

* *

SUNDAY SCHOOL TEACHER: THE THREE WISE MEN FOLLOWED A BIG STAR.

BOY: OH! THEY WERE LIKE BIBLICAL PAPARAZZI.

* *

Teacher: Michelangelo painted the Sistine Chapel on his back. Isn't that amazing?
Boy: Big Deal. My uncle is a sailor and he had a battleship tattooed on his chest.

Teacher: I heard you went to the Grand Canyon on vacation. What did you think of it?
Girl: It was just gorges.

Teacher: Does anyone know Samuel Clemens' pen name?
Boy: No. And we don't know the name of his pencil either.

CHAPTER **2**

Farm Funnies

Why did the herd of sheep call the police?
They'd been fleeced by a con man.

Why did Mr. Duck get arrested?
The police caught him quacking a safe.

What do you call a hen from Georgia who changes the color of her feathers?
Southern dyed chicken.

What do you get if you cross an armored military vehicle with a sheep?
Tank ewe.

What do you call a cow that always has bad luck?
A barn loser.

What do you get if you cross a toad and a pig?

A wart hog.

● ●

Why couldn't the good egg lend the poor rooster five bucks?

Because the egg was broke.

● ● ● ● ● ● ● ● ● ● ●

Bunny Breeder: **Some of my rabbits are kind of old.**

Dairy Farmer: **Having a few gray hares is nothing to be ashamed of.**

What do you get if you put a dairy cow in a garden?
Milkweed.

What do you get if you cross a hog with a frog?

A hamphibian.

● ● ● ● ● ● ● ● ●

What is a pig's favorite ballet?

Swine Lake.

● ● ● ● ● ● ● ● ● ● ●

LESTER: IS SHAKESPEARE THE REAL NAME OF YOUR HOG?

CHESTER: NAH. IT'S JUST HIS PEN NAME.

What do you get if you cross a lemon grove and a herd of cows?

Lots of sour cream.

What do you get if you cross a cow with a tiger?

Something that's too dangerous to milk.

Rooster: Would you like to give a speech to the hens?

Duck: I'll take a quack at it.

* *

WHAT'S PIGSKIN USED FOR?

TO HOLD THE PIG TOGETHER.

* * * * * * * * * *

What do you get if you cross a pig and an angel?

Hog heaven.

* * * * * * * * * *

Why do cows give milk? They're not smart enough to sell it.

Mrs. Sheep: Anything interesting in tonight's newspaper?

Mr. Ram: No. It's all baaaad news.

Why are horses bad dancers?
They have two left feet.

• • • • • • • • • • • • • • • •

SIGN ON A ROAD TO A SHEEP FARM:

No ewe turns.

* * * * * * * * * * * * * *

Karate Pig: How'd you like a pork chop?
Boxer Sheep: No thanks. How'd you like a wool sock?
Tough Bunny: Knock it off before I rabbit punch both of you.

* *

DAFFY DEFINITION:
Goat Herder: A person who likes to work with kids.

* *

WHAT DID CAPTAIN CATTLE SAY TO
SERGEANT STEER?
LET'S BEEF UP OUR DEFENSES.

What do you get if you cross a hog and a Texas lawman?

A pork ranger.

• •

THEN THERE WAS THE DAIRY COW THAT STARTED A LAWN-MOOING BUSINESS.

• •

What sound do you hear when you cross a cow with an owl?

Moo-who.

• •

What did the umpire yell when the pig slid into home?

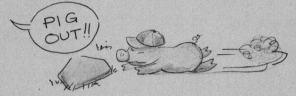

"Pig out!"

• •

Tex: Was the All-Steer band any good?
Rex: Not really, but they had a good horn section.

What do you get if you put a sheep in a steam room?

A wool sweater.

Where do the Rockette Cow dancers perform?

Radio City Moosic Hall.

Man: What do you do for a living?

Farmer: I raise female pigs and male deer.

Man: Is that profitable?

Farmer: I already have one hundred sows and bucks.

What's the best way to keep milk fresh?

Leave it in the cow.

FARMER: HOW IS MY SICK HORSE?

VET: HE'S IN STABLE CONDITION.

What does a rooster
on a dairy farm
shout at dawn?

Cock-a-doodle moo!

Why did the nanny
goat quit her job?
She had too many kids to take care of.

What do you get if you cross a flock of woolly
animals and angels?
Sheep in heavenly peace.

****

Where do young cows eat their lunch?
In a calf-eteria.

Shepherd #1: I heard wolves attack
flocks at night.
Shepherd #2: So have I, but I'm not
losing any sheep over it.

Did you hear about the two shepherds who became best friends even though they had mutton in common?

* * * * * * * * * * * * * * * * *

What has four wheels, two horns, and gives milk?
A cow on a skateboard.

* *

WHAT DO YOU CALL A PIG THAT ROBS HOUSES?

A HAM BURGLAR.

* * * * * * * * * * * * * * * *

Where does a ham burglar go if he gets caught?

To the state pen.

* *

Why couldn't the dairy cow give milk?
She was an udder failure.

What's the easiest way to count your farm animals?
Use a cowculator.

* * * * * * * * * * * * * * * *

Where do bovines go to enjoy fun in the sun?
Cowlifornia.

* *

WHAT DO YOU GET WHEN A HERD OF DAIRY COWS IS CAUGHT IN AN EARTHQUAKE?

MILKSHAKES.

* *

What did Mr. Pig say to Ms. Hog?

"I wanna hold your ham."

What do you call a pig that gets fired from its job?
A canned ham.

What did the hog say after it laid in the hot sun too long?
"I'm bacon out here."

• • • • • • • • • • • • • • • •

SIGN ON A
PIG STY:
Visitor porking only.

• • • • • • • • • • • • • • • •

What do you call a
royal castle owned
by a male deer and a
little pig?
Buck and Ham Palace.

****

What do you get if you cross a shelled nut with a ram?
A peanut butter.

What does a pig eat on a hot day?
A slopsicle.

What did the sheep say to the ram?
Hey, move your butt!

What hen was the first chicken in space?
Cluck Rogers.

Why did Mr. Pig go to the casino?
He wanted to play the slop machines.

What do you get when a pig falls down a steep hill?
Pork roll.

THEN THERE WERE THE NEWLYWED HORSES THAT CHECKED INTO THE BRIDAL SUITE.

Mack: I heard you wrote a book about how to stop a stampede of wild horses.
Zack: Yes. It's a tale of whoa.

What's the quickest way to ship a small horse?
Use pony express.

Billy: When your young thoroughbred colt grows into a horse, are you going to race him?
Willy: Heck no! He's already faster than I am.

What did Barbie do when she directed the hens in a play?
Barbie cued the chickens.

When do baby hens leave their hotel?
At chickout time.

Farmer: I own a skunk farm.
Reporter: Now that's a stinkin' way to earn a living.

Poultry farmer: I bought fifty mail-order baby chickens and they haven't arrived yet.
Sales clerk: Relax. The chicks are in the mail.

FARMER: DO YOU WANT TO HEAR HOW I STARTED MY RABBIT FARM?
REPORTER: NO. I DON'T CARE FOR HARE-RAISING TALES.

Where do sheep get their hair cut?
At the local baa-baa shop.

SIGN ON A
CHICKEN COOP:
No fowl language!

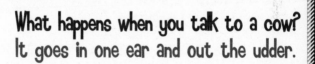

Why didn't the
rooster cross the
road?
Because deep
down he was
really a chicken.

What happens when you talk to a cow?
It goes in one ear and out the udder.

What does a bison bet in Las Vegas?
Buffalo chips.

NOTICES:
Computer sheep use ewe tube.
Cows have Hay-T-M cards.
Crows have cawling cards.
Cavalry horses have charge cards.

▲▲▲▲▲▲▲▲▲▲▲▲▲▲▲▲▲▲▲▲▲▲▲▲▲▲▲▲

How does a poultry farmer keep track of newborn chickens? He makes notes in his chick book.

▼▼▼▼▼▼▼▼▼▼▼▼▼▼▼▼▼▼

ZEKE: I KNOW A HOG THAT ATE 100 DILL CUCUMBERS.

DEKE: THAT'S QUITE A PICKLED PIG'S FEAT.

▼▼▼▼▼▼▼▼▼▼▼▼▼▼▼▼▼▼▼▼▼▼▼▼▼▼▼▼▼▼

Mother Hen to her chicks at midnight: "Now go to sleep and I don't want to hear another peep out of you."

WHAT DO YOU FIND AT A HOG MALL?
PORK SHOPS.

What do you get if you cross a pig with a fir tree?
A porky pine.

What did the pig marshal say to the hog outlaw?
"Reach for the sty, pardner."

CHAPTER **3**

Ghoulish Giggles & Weirdo Witches

Who do you call to clean a filthy haunted house?
The Ghost Dusters.

Ghostbuster: How much will you charge to haunt my teacher?
Ghost: For ten bucks I'll scare the wits out of him.
Ghostbuster: Here's five dollars to do the job. My teacher's a half-wit.

Harry: I'm tired of studying magic.
Wizard: Maybe you should rest a spell.

What feat did the ghoul gymnast perform?
He did a cemetery vault.

What did the ghoul say when he saw a new grave?
Yo! I can dig it.

Why did the ghost go to the pond?
He was a duck haunter.

"Booo!"

Why did the ghosts go to the baseball game?
To boo the umpire.

What do you get if you cross Bambi with a ghost?
Bamboo.

What's green, slimy, and scares people?

Kermit the Boo-Frog.

NOTICE: Fashionable ghosts wear designer boo jeans.

How do you measure a cemetery?
Use a graveyard stick.

What kind of craft does a space ghost fly?
A BOO-F-O.

PSYCHOLOGIST: WHY ARE YOU SAD, MS. SKELETON?

MS. SKELETON: I HAVE NO BODY TO LOVE.

What do you get if you cross a ghoul with a cobbler?
A creep shoe.

Boy Ghost: What game do you want to play?
Girl Ghost: Hide and shriek!

Why did the ghosts go to the hospital?
To have his ghoulstones removed.

* * * * * * * * *

WHY DON'T GHOSTS STAR
IN COWBOY MOVIES?
BECAUSE THEY ALWAYS
SPOOK THE HORSES.

* * * * * * * * * * * * * *

What does a creepy person get when he learns to fly?
A high ghoul diploma.

Which creepy general was the victor of the monsters' civil war?

Gholysses S. Grant.

Witch: The stick of my magic broom is broken.

Wizard: Don't worry, I'll handle it.

Ghost pirate: How will I know where the treasure is buried?
Sea witch: That's easy. Hex marks the spot.

What kind of horse does a cowboy ghost ride?
A night mare.

Mother Witch to Daughter: If you don't study hard at charm school, you'll never learn to spell correctly.

* * * * * * * * * * * * * *

What kind of weapon does a witch from space use?
A hex-ray gun.

I'VE SET IT TO "TOAD!"

WHAT DO YOU GET IF YOU CROSS A GHOST AND A SMALL PURPLE FLOWER?

A SHRIEKING VIOLET.

• •

What do you get when you cross cheddar cheese with a sorcerer?
Cheese Whiz.

• •

Boy: How did you get a role in that new ghost movie?

Girl: I did well in the scream test.

• •

How did the ghost keep his haunted house?

In a frightful mess.

• •

What do ghosts eat with roast beef and gravy?
Monster mash potatoes.

What does a construction ghost drive?
A boodozer.

NOTICE: Most ghouls work the graveyard shift.

What did the
ghost monster
say to the
alphabet?
I come to eat U.

WHAT DO YOU CALL A GHOST WHO
HAUNTS A HOTEL?

AN INN SPECTRE.

KOOKY QUESTION: Do witch
computers have spell check?

What do you get if you cross the
Ice Age with a witch?
A long cold spell.

What happens if you don't pay your exorcist on time?

You get repossessed.

How did the witch teacher grade her pupils' spelling tests?

She used a magic marker.

What do you get if you cross a witch doctor with morning mist?

Voodew.

NOTICE: Most ghosts like spiritual music.

What do baby ghosts wear on their feet?

Boo-ties.

What do you call a spook who uses public transportation?

A ghost busser.

WHO IS SPOOKY AND HAUNTS MOTHER GOOSE LAND?

LITTLE BOO PEEP.

What happens when a little ghost falls down at the playground?

He gets a boo-boo.

What is a creep's favorite holiday?

April Ghoul's Day.

What did the ghost driver do when the traffic light turned red?
He screeched to a stop.

What did the witch say to the people of Salem, Massachusetts? You folks really burn me up.

****

What colors are the ghost flag of America?
Red, white, and boooo!

****

What do you call a monster gopher?
A ghoul digger.

What does a witch order while staying in a hotel?
Broom service.

What do you call a ghoul protest?
A demon-stration.

WHAT DO YOU GET IF YOU CROSS AN EVIL WOMAN WHO CASTS MAGIC SPELLS WITH CORRODED METAL?
THE WICKED WITCH OF THE RUST.

Zelda: I know a hexed number.
Nelda: Witch one?
Zelda: That's right.

****

What do you get if you cross a dinosaur with a witch's spell?

Tyrannosaurus Hex.

• • • • • • • • • • • • • • • • • • • •

Vampire: What kind of mouthwash do you use?
Witch: Brand Hex.

• • • • • • • • • • • • • • • • • • • •

How do you unlock a haunted house?
Use a skeleton key.

What is the ghost anthem of America?
Three scares for the red, white, and boo.

Why shouldn't a witch on a broomstick lose her temper?
She might fly off the handle.

Who checks haunted houses?
The building in-spectre.

What did the friendly geek ghost say?
Don't be afraid of the dork.

WHAT DO YOU FIND ON THE WINDOWS OF A HAUNTED HOUSE?
SHUDDERS.

What is a ghost's favorite month?
Februscary.

● ● ● ● ● ● ● ● ● ● ● ● ● ● ● ●

**What month were
most ghosts born?**
Shocktober.

● ● ● ● ● ● ● ● ● ● ● ● ● ● ● ●

Why was the witch
so thirsty?
She just had a dry spell.

● ● ● ● ● ● ● ● ● ● ● ● ●

**What do you call two young witches
who share a dorm room?
Broom mates.**

What did the witch say to her
broom at bedtime?
Sweep dreams.

How do you make a haunted house more creepy?
Turn on the scare conditioner.

What do you get if you cross hot oil with a wizard?
A frying sorcerer.

WHAT DO YOU FEED A BABY WITCH?

A MAGIC FORMULA.

What did the little girl ghost get for her birthday?
A haunted dollhouse.

What's a cold evil candle called?
The Wicked Wick of the North.

Why do witches wear nametags?
So they know which witch
is which.

• •

Who does all of the talking at a
ghost press conference?
The spooksperson.

• •

WHAT IS SPOOKIER THAN THE OUTSIDE OF
A HAUNTED HOUSE?

THE INSIDE.

• •

Why won't a witch wear a
flat hat?
Because it's pointless.

CHAPTER
4
Wacky Waiters

Table for Juan!

Knock! Knock!
Who's there?
Menu.
Menu who?
Menu wish upon a star.

Knock! Knock!
Who's there?
Pasta.
Pasta who?
Pasta salt and pepper.

* * * * * * * * * * * * * *

What do you get if you cross a waiter with a soldier?
A person who knows how to take and follow orders.

* * * * * * * * * * * * * *

Customer: I'm so hungry I could eat a horse.
Waiter: Well, sir, you certainly came to the right place.

Customer: I'm in the mood for a tasty meal. What would you recommend?
Waiter: I recommend you try another restaurant.

CUSTOMER: UGH! THIS IS THE WORST MEAL I'VE HAD IN TWO WEEKS.
WAITER: WHERE DID YOU EAT TWO WEEKS AGO, MISS?
CUSTOMER: RIGHT HERE!

Knock! Knock!
Who's there?
Peas Pasta
Peas Pasta who?
Peas Pasta grated cheese.

SIGN ON A TRUCK STOP: We fill your tank and your tummy with gas.

Knock! Knock!
Who's there?
Hal.
Hal who?
Hal have the blue plate special.

▼▼▼▼▼▼▼▼▼▼▼▼▼▼▼▼▼▼▼▼▼▼▼▼▼▼▼

Chef: *Why are you running?*
Waiter: *The big guy at table four wants rushin' dressing.*

▲▲▲▲▲▲▲▲▲▲▲▲▲▲▲▲▲▲▲▲▲▲▲▲▲▲▲

Customer: Waiter, is the fish on this plate fresh?
Waiter: If it were any fresher sir, it would be swimming in your water glass.

▼▼▼▼▼▼▼▼▼▼▼▼▼▼▼▼▼▼▼▼▼▼▼▼▼▼▼

Customer: Why do they call this place the canoe diner?

Waiter: There's no tipping allowed.

▲▲▲▲▲▲▲▲▲▲▲▲▲▲▲▲▲▲▲▲▲▲▲▲▲▲▲

Customer: I'd like to have a pork chop, and make it lean.
Waiter. Yes, sir. In which direction?

Where do tennis players go for lunch?
To a food court.

What did Peter order at the Neverland Italian Restaurant?
Pan Pizza.

● ●

CUSTOMER #1: HOW'S THE SERVICE IN THIS DINER?
CUSTOMER #2: TERRIBLE. IT TAKES THEM AN HOUR TO SERVE A MINUTE STEAK.

Customer: Why is this place called the Underwater Diner?
Waiter: Sub sandwiches are our specialty.

● ● ● ● ● ● ● ● ● ● ● ●

What did the waiter shout when John went into the Mexican food restaurant?
Table for Juan!

Table for Juan!

SIGN IN A DINER:
Early Bird Special:
Roast Spring Chicken.

• • • • • • • • • • • • • • • • • • • •

Customer: Hey waiter! I've been waiting an hour for the turtle soup I ordered.

Waiter: I'm sorry, sir, but you know how slow turtles are.

AND NOW THERE'S A HARE IN IT!

• • • • • • • • • • •

Knock! Knock!

Who's there?

Aspect?

Aspect who?

Aspect to get free bread with my meal.

• • • • • • • • • • • • • • • • • • • •

French waiter: Would you like to try some snails?

American Customer: No thanks. I prefer fast food.

Customer: **I see you have tomato soup on your menu.**
Waiter: **Yes, sir. Is that what you'd like to have?**
Customer: **No. I'd like to have a clean menu.**

✳ ✳ ✳ ✳ ✳ ✳ ✳ ✳ ✳

Knock! Knock!
Who's there?
Sid.
Sid who?
Sid down and a waiter will take your order.

CUSTOMER: HOW DO YOU MAKE YOUR FAMOUS GOLD SOUP?
WAITER: WE START OUT BY PUTTING IN 14 CARROTS.

Waiter: Would you like to try our Porterhorse steak special?
Customer: Don't you mean Porterhouse steak?
Waiter: If you say so, sir.

Customer: Waiter, this apple pie tastes fishy. Waiter: That's impossible, sir. It's crabapple pie.

CHAPTER **5**

The Merry Military

Knock! Knock!
Who's there?
Navy.
Navy who?
Navy we'll meet again someday.

ATTENTION: THE U.S. ARMY SEEKS CLEANING PERSONNEL FOR MOP-UP OPERATIONS.

Where does a smart general hide his armies?

In his sleevies.

Why did the dentist join the Marines? He wanted to be a drill sergeant.

ON MY COMMAND, SPIT!

Knock! Knock!
Who's there?
Army.
Army who?
Army and my friends invited to your party?

• •

What is a soldier's least favorite month?

March.

• •

What did Captain Skunk say to his soldiers?

Follow my odors, men.

• •

What makes a soldier's foot hurt?
Boot cramp.

• • • • • • • • • • •

What did the soldier say to his Army blanket?
Cover me, pal.

Why do vampires hate all Marines?
Because they're tough leathernecks.

• •

WHAT DO CARRIER PILOTS PLAY CARDS WITH?

A FLIGHT DECK.

• •

Captain: Would you like me to give your outfit some armored vehicles?

Soldier: Yes, sir. A million tanks!

• •

Mack: Do you fly a jet fighter?

Zack: No, I bailed out of pilot school.

• •

What did the soldier say to the football quarterback?

Can I have a weekend pass?

• •

Mother: Is that the cafeteria where you have your meals?

Soldier: Yes, mom, but it's a mess.

Mother: Well, someone should clean it up.

Sarge: My troop has been drilling in the hot sun for hours.
Captain: I can tell. They have marching odors.

Knock! Knock!
Who's there?
I, Major.
I, Major who?
I, Major bed for you.

****

Sarge: Shoulder arms!
Soldier: Is this a drill or an anatomy
          lesson?

****

How does a chicken
join the Army?
She signs
henlistment papers.

Knock! Knock!
Who's there?
A Moe.
A Moe who?
A Moe is what a gun shoots.

WHY DID THE CROW JOIN THE MARINES?

HE ANSWERED THE CAW OF DUTY.

What do you call volunteers for the Munchkin Armed Forces?
Army weecruits.

What did the paratrooper say to the parachute maker?

Please. Just chute me.

What do you get when a lumberjack joins the Air Force?
A chopper pilot.

What did the brave
baby soldier get?
A goo
conduct medal.

▼▼▼▼▼▼▼▼▼▼▼▼

Where does a
pilot keep his
flying suit?
On a plain hanger.

▲▲▲▲▲▲▲▲▲▲▲▲▲▲▲▲▲▲▲▲▲▲▲▲▲▲▲▲▲

Why did the soldiers shoot into the
burning building?
They were taught to fight fire
with fire.

▲▲▲▲▲▲▲▲▲▲▲▲▲▲▲▲▲▲▲▲▲▲▲▲▲▲▲

WHAT DO SOLDIERS HUM?

PLA-TUNES.

▼▼▼▼▼▼▼▼▼▼▼▼▼▼▼▼▼▼▼▼▼▼▼▼▼▼▼▼▼

Knock! Knock!
Who's there?
A band.
A band who?
A band on ship men. We're sinking!

Why did the orange become a sailor?
He wanted to be in a navel battle.

▲▲▲▲▲▲▲▲▲▲▲▲▲▲▲▲▲▲▲▲▲▲▲▲▲▲▲▲▲▲

How did the sailor get knocked out?
Someone decked him.

▼▼▼▼▼▼▼▼▼▼▼

What did the
balding drill
sergeant say
to his hair?
Fall out!

FALL OUT!

▲▲▲▲▲▲▲▲▲▲▲▲▲▲▲▲▲▲▲▲▲▲▲▲▲▲▲▲▲▲

Why did the pooch train to become a pilot?
He wanted to have some aerial dogfights.

▲▲▲▲▲▲▲▲▲▲▲▲▲▲▲▲▲▲▲▲▲▲▲▲▲▲▲▲▲▲

SERGEANT: REMEMBER SOLDIER, YOUR
RIFLE IS YOUR BEST FRIEND.
SOLDIER: GOSH SARGE, I COULD
NEVER FIRE MY BEST FRIEND.

What do rabbit pilots fly?
Hare combat missions.

What do you get if you cross a razor and a rifle?
A sharp shooter.

* * * * * * *

What large reptile do you find on a Navy ship?
The navi-gator.

* * * * * * *

Man #1: I'm an Army doctor.
Man #2: Do you treat officers?
Man #1: No. I have a private practice.

Where do machine guns hatch their babies?
In machine gun nests.

Why do pilots like Kansas and Oklahoma?
They're great planes states.

Where did
Soldier Santa
take cover?
In a fox ho ho-ho!

* * * * * * * * * * * * * * *

What do you get if you cross soldiers
and locomotive engineers?
Army training.

* * * * * * * * * * * * * * *

Clerk: Why are you hiring so many
ex-military men?

Manager: I'm expecting a price war.

Girl: Were you in the Vietnam War?
Grandfather: Yes. I put up a good fight, but they drafted me anyway.

Knock! Knock!
Who's there?
G.I.
G.I. who?
G.I. don't really care.

Soldier: Should I wrap the bandolier of bullets around my belly, Sarge.
Sarge: No solider. Don't waist your ammo.

What did the sergeant say after his soldiers jumped into their bunks?
Cover yourselves, men!

What did the Green Giant wear after he joined the Navy?
A pea coat.

WHAT DID THE BIG OCTOPUS SOLDIER SAY TO THE LITTLE OCTOPUS SOLDIER?
YOU'RE A SMALL ARMS EXPERT, AREN'T YOU?

Why couldn't the Army Captain go to the show?
It was general admission only.

CHAPTER
6
Silly Superheroes

Why did the judge order Superman to be held in jail until his case could be heard?
Because he was a flight risk.

WHICH SUPERHEROES DO YOU FIND ON A GOLF COURSE?
THE FANTASTIC FOURSOME.

What do you get if you cross a superhero with a fish?
A caped cod.

Where does Bruce Wayne wash up?
In his bat tub.

What is Aquaman's part-time job?
He owns a sub shop.

Who do you get if you cross Bruce Wayne with a geek?
Batman, the Dork Knight.

What do you get if you cross a hangman's knot with a very fast superhero?
A noose flash.

* * * * * * * * * * * * * *

What did the Hulk eat for lunch?
A six-foot comic-book-hero sandwich.

* * * * * * * * * * * * * * * *

What do you call a masked crime fighter who has no personality?
A super zero.

* * * * * * * * * * * * * * * * * * *

Where did Boy Torch meet Girl Torch?
On match.com.

* * * * * * * *

What is Super Fish's secret identity?
Carp Kent.

* * * * * * * * * * * * * * * * *

What is Barkman's secret identity?
Spruce Wayne.

WHY DIDN'T WOLVERINE GET LONG NAILS
WHEN HE FIRST SIGNED ON TO BE A
SUPERHERO?
THERE WAS NO CLAUSE IN HIS ORIGINAL
CONTRACT.

* * * * * * * * * * * * *

Who works with Batman and floats in the ocean.
Robin, the Buoy Wonder.

* * * * * * * * * * * * *

How quick is Super Ox?
He's faster than a speeding bullock.

* * * * * * * * * * * * * * * * *

What kind of vehicle does Captain Genius drive?
A think tank.

* * * * * * * * * * * * * * * * *

What do you get if you cross the Human Torch with Aquaman?
A heat wave.

Knock! Knock!
Who's there?
Ozzie.
Ozzie who?
Ozzie through brick walls with my X-ray vision.

SPIDEY: HOW DO I GET THESE WRINKLES OUT OF MY SUPERHERO COSTUME?
THOR: IRON, MAN!

Mack: This big sandwich tastes like paper.
Zack: Maybe it's a comic book hero.

Knock! Knock!
Who's there?
Dish.
Dish who?
Dish looks like a job for Superman!

• •

What does Spider Guy use to take pictures?
A web cam.

ATTENTION: The Super Torch is full of hot air.

• • • • • • • • • • • • • •

Who is Super Ghost? He's a crime frighter.

• • • • • • • • • • • • • • • • • •

What kind of hero goes out in a snowstorm? One that has super plowers.

• •

What do you find in the home of a comic-book artist? Wall-to-wall paneling.

Villain: Spider Pig, I've discovered your secret identity.
Spider Pig: Please don't squeal on me.

What happened to the evil villain Mr. Elastic?
He's doing a ten-year stretch in the state pen.

PUNNY SUPERHEROES

CAPTAIN KANGAROO – He leaps tall buildings in a single bound.

MR. MATH MARVEL – He'll solve the crime even if clues don't add up.

DR. CARDIAC MAN – He knows what evil lurks in the hearts of men.

LOTTERY LASS – Crooks have no chance of winning when she's around.

WHAT DO YOU GET IF YOU CROSS A GIANT BEE WITH CLARK KENT?
BUZZARO SUPERMAN.

▼▼▼▼▼▼▼▼▼▼▼▼▼▼▼▼▼▼▼▼▼▼▼▼▼▼▼

What do you get if you cross snobby teens with Bruce Wayne's vehicle?
The Bratmobile.

Where does a villain go to get a knuckle sandwich?
A fist-food restaurant.

Knock! Knock!
Who's there?
Izzy.
Izzy who?
Izzy a good guy or a bad guy?

▲▲▲▲▲▲▲▲▲▲▲▲

Why did Super Girl go out with the Human Torch? She thought he was hot.

▼▼▼▼▼▼▼▼▼▼▼▼▼▼▼▼▼▼▼▼▼▼▼▼

What crow has super powers?
Captain Americaw.

MORE PUNNY SUPERHEROES

CAPTAIN BLABBERMOUTH – He's no longer in the superhero business because he told everyone his secret identity.

SUPER SURFER CHICK – She can end a crime wave before it starts.

SUPER CYCLOPS – He keeps an eye out for trouble.

SERGEANT RAZOR BLADE – He always arrives in the knick of time.

THE FANTASTIC EGGMAN – No crook can beat him.

What do you call uncanny super cats?

Mewtants.

Crook: How do you turn Batman
into Splatman?
Robber: Knock him out and push him off
a tall building.

Spider Guy: Iron Dude, how did you let
that crook escape?
Iron Dude: I've been out of the
superhero biz for a while and I guess
I'm a bit rusty.

Knock! Knock!
Who's there?
One deer.
One deer who?
One deer woman to the
rescue!

WHAT HAS FOUR WHEELS, FLIES, AND
HAS AMAZING POWERS?
SUPER VAN.

What do you call a person who shows you around Asgard, the home of the Norse thunder god?
A Thor guide.

WHICH SUPERHERO CRIME FIGHTER ENJOYS MAKING BAD JOKES?
THE PUN-ISHER.

Which team of gag writers pens the best superhero puns?
The Joker and the Riddler.

Which superhero battles evil chicken thieves?
The Eggs Men.

What did Robin say to Bruce Wayne at bath time?
Can I borrow your bat robe?

Where do superheroes play baseball?
In the Justice League.

• •

WHY DID THE BOY INVITE BATMAN TO
HIS MIDDAY MEAL?
HE WANTED TO HAVE A HERO FOR
LUNCH.

• •

Why did the masked crime fighter roll after the escaping villain?
Because he was a marble superhero.

• •

What
sheep is a
superhero?
Baaman.

CHAPTER
7
For the Birds

What's black and
white and
red all over?
A sloppy
penguin eating
tomato soup.

* * * * * * * * * * * * *

WHAT DO GEESE DO WHEN THEY
GET CAUGHT IN A TRAFFIC JAM?

THEY HONK A LOT.

* * * * * * * * * * * *

Who do you get if you cross a water fowl
with a western hero of the O.K. Corral?

Duck Holiday.

* * * * * * * * * * * * * * * *

**What do you get if you cross an
eagle and a minister?**
A bird of pray.

What do you get if you cross pigeons
in a coop with pigs?
Roost pork.

Why didn't the nervous rooster cross the road? Down deep he really was really a chicken.

* * * * * * *

WHAT DO YOU GET IF YOU CROSS A ROOSTER WITH A PARROT?
A BIRD THAT YELLS, "GET UP!" AT THE CRACK OF DAWN.

* * * * * * * * * * * * * *

Society Sue: My pet canary is so spoiled she refuses to sing unless she's accompanied by a pianist.

Snobby Robbie: My pet dog is so spoiled, when I command him to sit, our butler has to pull out a chair for him.

* * * * * * * * * * * * * * * * * *

What did Ms. Flamingo say to Mr. Crane? Quit storking me.

Why couldn't Mr. Goose buy a house?
He didn't have a down payment.

* * * * * * * * * * * * * * * * * * *

Which bird
skydives out of
airplanes?
The parrot
trooper.

* * * * * * * * * * *

Hen: I don't have
much of a nest egg.
Duck: Why is that?
Hen: Because all of my life I've worked for
chicken feed.

* *

What does a bird maid use to keep the nest clean?
A feather duster.

* * * * * * * * * * * * * *

What happens when pigeons
have a hot coop?
They roost themselves.

NOTICE: Acme Bird Phones—
We tweet you right!

Ollie: I'm a wise old owl.
Robin: So, who gives a hoot?

DAFFY DEFINITION:
Bird nest: Cheep housing.

HOW DOES A CROW KNOW WHO'S TRYING
TO CONTACT HIM?

HE CHECKS HIS CAWLER I.D.

What kind of bird
insults people?

A mockingbird.

Where did the little bird go after
elementary school?
To junior fly school.

Why was Mr. Duck upset?
His bill was in the mail.

What did Ms. Duck get after her nose job?

A big medical bill.

What game do mother hens play with their chicks?
Peck a boo.

NOTICE: Buy a duck feather iPod and get free down loads.

WHICH BIRD WORKS AT THE CONSTRUCTION SITE?

THE CRANE.

What birds work underground.
Coal mynas.

Mr. Pigeon: I need to go out tonight.
Mrs. Pigeon: Why?
Mr. Pigeon: I've been cooped up at home all week.

What has feathers and holds up banks?
A robber ducky.

What do you call a couple of keets?
Parakeets.

WHAT DO YOU GET IF YOU CROSS A TORTOISE AND A PIGEON?

A TURTLE DOVE.

What do you get if you cross ducks with popcorn?
Quacker Jacks.

What do you call a baby bird?

A chirp off the old block.

- - - - - - - - - - - - - - - - -

Mr. Duck: Are those new feathers?

Mr. Goose: No. It's hand me down.

- - - - - - - - - - - - - - - - -

What do you call an in air
collision between two birds?
A feather bender.

- - - - - - - - - - - - - - - - -

What's black and white and red on the bottom?

A baby penguin with diaper rash.

- - - - - - - - - - - - - - - - -

Worm #1: What's
the best way to
avoid getting eaten
by an early bird?
Worm #2: Sleep late.

What do you get if you cross a canary
with a chimp?
A chirp monk.

* *

When does a black bird seek
psychiatric help?
When it's a raven maniac.

* * * * * * * * * * * * * * * * * * * *

What did the crow say when he saw
three ears of corn?

Humm ... which one should I peck?

* *

What do you get if you cross a
magician and a canary?
A trick or tweeter.

What do you get when
geese fly headfirst into a brick
wall?

Goose bumps.

WHAT HAS
FEATHERS AND
PLAYS JAZZ
MUSIC?
A DUCKSEY-
LAND BAND.

* *

What did the old tree say to the sapsucker?

Quick pecking on me.

* *

Jack: **Why are those storks flying so fast?**
Mack: **Maybe they're hurry cranes.**

* *

Mr. Vulture: What's for dinner?
Mrs. Vulture: Leftovers.

* *

DAFFY DEFINITIONS:

Condor: A prison entrance.

Goblet: A baby turkey.

What do you get when you clone a duck and cross the results with a hoagie?

A double ducker sandwich.

* * * * * * * * * * * * * *

What did the mallard wear to his wedding?

A duckcedo.

* * * * * * * *

What do you get if you cross a zebra and a penguin? An animal in a striped tuxedo.

* * * * * * * * * * *

CHAPTER
8
Funny Money

What kind of books
does a banker
like to read?
Check books.

CHECKS
AND
BALANCE
SHEETS

****

WHAT DO YOU GET IF YOU CROSS A
MORTGAGE COMPANY AND A SONGWRITER?

BANK NOTES.

**How did the bankrupt
hay farmers survive?**
The government baled them out.

Where does a bad taxi
driver keep his money?

In a crash register.

****

*How do you pay a lumberyard owner
for the boards you ordered?*
Write him a plank check.

Then there was the art gallery that got into financial trouble because its account was overdrawn.

What is a kangaroo check?
It's one that bounces at the bank.

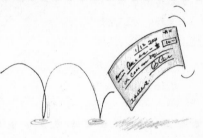

Knock! Knock!
Who's there?
Iowa.
Iowa who?
Iowa lot of money to my creditors.

****

Bill: Do you like being a professional field-goal kicker?
Will: It helps me foot my bills.

What do you get if you cross a ten-dollar bill with a parrot?
Money that talks.

Why did the investor throw his money into the river? He wanted to check his cash flow.

WHY DID THE LITTLE BUG PAY THE DOG A DOLLAR?

IT WAS A RENTAL FLEA.

ATTENTION: **Moses had an excellent prophet-sharing plan.**

STUPID STOCK TIP:
Use your disposable income to invest in garbage trucks.

How did the beekeeper get started selling honey?
He got a buzzness loan from the bank.

YOUR ATTENTION PLEASE:
Yard Sale – buy this lot!
Garage Sale – parked cars not included.
Moving Sale – items are going fast.
Block Sale – square deals.

● ● ● ● ● ● ● ● ● ● ● ● ● ● ● ● ● ● ● ●

Bob: Why should I put my money into Acme vaults?

Rob: It's a safe investment.

● ● ● ● ● ● ● ● ● ● ● ● ● ● ● ● ● ● ● ●

BOB: WHY SHOULD I PURCHASE AIRLINE STOCK?

ROB: IT'S A HIGH YIELD INVESTMENT.

● ● ● ● ● ● ● ● ● ● ● ● ● ● ● ● ● ● ● ●

Gary: How's your job at the bank?
Larry: Good. I'm really cleaning up.
Gary: Are you a loan officer?
Larry: No. I'm a maintenance man.

● ● ● ● ● ● ● ● ● ● ● ● ● ● ● ● ● ● ● ●

Jack: I produce charcoal for a living.
Mack: How's business?
Jack: It's always in the black.

KNOCK! KNOCK!
WHO'S THERE?
ALONE.
ALONE WHO?
ALONE FROM A BANK IS WHAT YOU
NEED TO BUY A HOUSE.

NOTICES:

Invest in our school for mimes.
Silent partners are most welcome.

Invest in a poultry farm.
We have a layaway program.

Invest in rare, old comic books.
We are not a collection agency.

Mr. Good: I sell religious songbooks.
Mr. Sims: Is there a big market for
your product?
Mr. Good: Yes. We have a lot of
hymn-pulse buyers.

Mr. Jones: Why did you demolish
that structure?
Worker: I thought the building
deserved a raze.

Ike: I sell barbells
and weights.
Spike: How's
business?
Ike: Sales have
been weak.

Bill: *I'm a refrigeration expert.*
Will: *That sounds like cool work.*
Bill: *Not really. We're having a*
pay freeze.

Man: Are there any job openings?
Unemployment Agency: I'm sorry,
but the job market is currently
flooded.
Man: That's great news! I'm a
plumber.

**What do you get if you cross
a swimming pool with a
mortgage company?**
Dive-through banking.

WHAT DID THE PIER SAY TO THE SHIP
THAT ARRIVED LATE IN PORT?
NOW I'LL HAVE TO DOCK YOUR PAY.

Knock! Knock!
Who's there?
Welfare.
Welfare who?
Welfare crying out loud, I need
government assistance.

* * * * * * * * * * * *

**What do you get if you cross a
mortgage with morning mist?**
Monthly rent that's always dew.

* * * * * * * * * * * * * * * * * *

SIGN IN A FISH MARKET:
School Sale Today!

* * * * * * * * * * * * * * * * * *

ATTENTION: Used boats at sail prices.

CUSTOMER: WHY ARE YOUR
WRISTWATCHES SO EXPENSIVE?
CLERK: TIME IS MONEY.

Knock! Knock!
Who's there?
Minny.
Minny who?
Minny mum wage is low pay.

✱✱✱✱✱✱✱✱✱✱✱✱✱✱✱✱✱✱✱✱✱✱✱✱✱

Why did the store manager take a sword to work? He was going to slash some prices.

✱✱✱✱✱✱

Knock! Knock!
Who's there?
Urn.
Urn who?
Urn a living or you'll starve.

KOOKY QUESTION:
Does Moby Dick have a lot of credit cods?

How was the Big Bad Wolf able to retire early?
He always earned time and a huff.

● ●

Mike: I sell diet books.
Spike: Oh. So you make fast money.

● ●

CHAPTER

****9****

Occupational Hazards

What did Attila the Barbarian do after he lost his job? He collected hunemployment.

Why did you quit your job at the coffee shop?
They didn't offer me enough perks.

Mr. Smith: I invest in skyscrapers.
Mr. Jones: You must have a lot of high-interest accounts.

DAFFY DEFINITION:
ATM – A real money market.

NOTICE: Buy Acme camera phones – just picture yourself owning one.

WANTED: Person to plan charity events. Plenty of benefits.

• • • • • • • • • • • • • • • • • • • •

SIGN ON A BUNGEE CORD COMPANY:
Even when our sales are down, we always bounce back.

• • • • • • • • • • • • • • • • • • • •

MR. CHUBB: I GAINED TWENTY POUNDS OF BELLY FAT SINCE I BECAME A RICH BUSINESSMAN.
MR. SLIM: JUST THINK OF IT AS INDUSTRIAL WAIST.

• • • • • • • • • • • • • • • • • • • •

SILLY SALES PITCH:
Acme Footwear: Wouldn't you like to be in our shoes?

Show me a real hip dude who works below ground ... and I'll show you a cool miner.

Harry: Should I quit my job at the glue factory?
Barry: I suggest you stick with it.

* *

Harry: When it comes to cash, I'm like the banker on the great Ark.
Barry: What do you mean?
Harry: I have Noah money.

What do you call the owner of a flower shop who's frozen stiff and can't move a muscle?
The petrified florist.

SILLY SALES PITCH:
Acme Scuba Diving Tanks: Our business is a breath of fresh air.

* *

Two lumberjacks were standing in front of a tall tree and they were having a heated argument. "Back off," said one lumberjack to the other. "I saw it first."

Matt: How did you do on your carpenter's exam?

Pat: I nailed it!

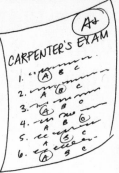

WANT ODDS

WANTED: Person to fill salt and pepper shakers at restaurant. Seasonal work.

WANTED: Cowboy to lasso steers. Must know the ropes and have lots of pull.

WANTED: Person to work in rearview mirror factory. Excellent hindsight a plus.

WANTED: Person to build playground equipment. Swing shifts.

WANTED: Contortionist needed to teach yoga class. Flexible hours.

MORE WANT ODDS

WANTED: Riding instructor with a sense of humor needed at equestrian school.

We want someone who will horse around with our students.

WANTED: Kennel needs pet exercisers willing to work until they're dog tired.

WANTED: Workers for sheep farm. We offer a profit-shearing plan.

WANTED: People needed to tend beehives. Our buzzword is success.

WANTED: Night watchman. If you're looking for security, this is the job for you.

WANTED: Electrician needed for light construction work. Must have current references.

What did the cast say to the bone?
Don't bother me now. I'm on my break.

Lester: Did you take a job working in the mine?
Chester: No. I got coal feet.

Show me a doctor who sets broken bones...and I'll show you a marrow minded person.

Who collects taxes owed to the Devil?
The Inferno Revenue Service.

THIS SHOULD ONLY TAKE AN ETERNITY!

ATTENTION:

Real Estate Agents are home schooled.

WANTED:
Assistant barber needed.
Part-time hours.

What do you call a person who makes miniature alarm clocks?

A small-time operator.

NOTICE! New plumbers needed. We'll make your pipe dreams come true.

NOTICE! Tailors needed. Come in for an interview so we can size you up.

What do you call a zombie who has two jobs?

A working stiff.

Why did Davy Jones hire a music teacher?

Because he wanted to tuna fish.

Sal: Do you like working as an exterminator?
Hal: No. It bugs me.

SILLY SLOGANS:

ACE PICTURE FRAMERS -
Let us hang around your house.

ACE CORN FARMS - Try our product
and you'll smile from ear to ear.

ACE YOGA CLASS -
We're your local limber yard.

ACE SHOELACES -
Tie us. You'll like us.

ACE SPORTS TARPS -
We cover all the bases.

ACE BELTS -
Let us hold up you.

Why was the new locksmith so successful on his first job?
Beginner's lock.

WANTED: SPACE EXPLORERS NEEDED. THE PAY IS OUT OF THIS WORLD!

What did the tired tree say to its boss?
I need a leaf of absence.

Why didn't the watchdog show up for guard duty?
He took a sic day.

* * * * * * * * * * * * * * *

Bart: I got a job gathering hens' eggs.
Art: Is it hard?
Bart: No. But I often have to work around the cluck.

EVEN MORE WANT ODDS

WANTED: Person to mop floors and dust ceilings. Must be willing to start from the bottom up.

WANTED: Assistant to archaeologist. Applicant must love the good old days.

WANTED: Person to work in burlap bag factory. No sack guarantee.

WANTED: Straight man to team with very funny comedian. No kidding around.

WANTED: Person to inflate balloons. The ideal candidate knows how to blow things out of proportion.

Knock! Knock!
Who's there?
Musk.
Musk who?
Musk you work late every
single night?

• • • • • • • • • • • • • • • • • • •

WHY ARE MOVIE DIRECTORS LIKE FISHERMEN?

BECAUSE THEY BOTH LIKE A PERFECT CAST.

• • • • • • • • • • • • • • • • • • •

What's the best way to sell math
problems to students?
Hire someone to run an add campaign.

• • • • • • • • • • • • • • • • • • •

How does a person become a
lumberjack?

First you have to pass an axe-am.

• • • • • • • • • • • • • • • • • • •

What did the frog foreman say to
his workers?
Let's get hopping, people.

What did the alligator foreman say to his workers?
Let's snap to it, men.

* * *

What did the dog foreman say to his crew?
Bark to work, fellas.

* * *

What did the centipede foreman say to his workers?
On your feet, feet, feet guys.

* * *

NOTICE:
WORK FOR ACME CANINE TRAINERS. WHEN YOU RETIRE FROM OUR COMPANY WE GIVE YOU A WATCHDOG.

Mr. Big: I'm the president of a lumber company.
Mr. Small: I bet you attend a lot of board meetings.

▲▲▲▲▲▲▲▲▲▲▲▲▲▲▲▲▲▲▲▲▲▲▲▲▲▲▲▲▲▲▲

LUMBERJACK #1: CAN I CHOP DOWN THAT OLD TREE?
LUMBERJACK #2: HEY! I AXED FIRST!

▼▼▼▼▼▼▼▼▼▼▼▼▼▼▼▼▼▼▼▼▼▼▼▼▼▼▼▼▼▼▼

What did the calendar say to its boss?
I need a day off.

▲▲▲▲▲▲▲▲▲▲▲▲▲▲▲▲▲▲▲▲▲▲▲▲▲▲▲▲▲

Knock! Knock!
Who's there?
Higher.
Higher who?
Higher the man in the pinstripe suit.

▲▲▲▲▲▲▲▲▲▲▲▲▲▲▲▲▲▲▲▲▲▲▲▲▲▲▲▲▲

What does a baker do when he wants to sleep late?
He puts up a donut disturb sign.

MORE SILLY SLOGANS:

ACME SOLAR VEHICLES – We're the hottest new car company under the sun.

ACME MUSIC STORE – Stop by at play time.

ACME STAIR COMPANY – Step up to a better life.

ACME CAR IGNITIONS – We start every day right.

ACME TAXI COMPANY – If you're feeling run down, let us pick you up.

ACME BATTERY COMPANY – We charge a little to charge you a lot.

▼▼▼▼▼▼▼▼▼▼▼▼▼▼▼▼▼▼▼▼▼▼▼▼▼▼▼▼▼

How did the first barber come to the United States?

He arrived on a clipper ship.

▲▲▲▲▲▲▲▲▲▲▲▲▲▲▲▲▲▲▲▲▲▲▲▲▲▲▲▲▲▲

Zack: I answered an ad that said surefire opportunity.
Mack: Did you get the job?
Zack: Yes. And then I got fired.

Why did the firemen rush to the forest?
Someone reported a tree-alarm fire.

* *

Publisher: So you wrote a book about a Scottish musical instrument?
Author: Yes. It's the story of my fife.

* * * * * * * * * * * * * *

What did the trumpet
player say to the
musician next to him?
I need to make a call.
Can I use your
sax-a-phone?

* * * * * * * * * * * * * *

ACME CANNON COMPANY–
Join our team while business
is booming. We never fire our
employees.

* *

How's your job at the compost
plant?

It's rotten work and the hours stink.

How's your job at the tire factory?
Wheel good, but tiring.

HOW'S YOUR JOB AT THE BREAD CRUMB PLANT?

IT'S GETTING STALE FAST.

How's your job at the travel agency?
It's going nowhere.

How's your job at the window plant?
It panes me to talk about it.

Why was the conductor crying?
His train was on a wailroad track.

WHAT DO YOU GET IF YOU CROSS A HIP-HOP SINGER WITH A TRAVELING SALESMAN?

SOMEONE WHO RAPS AT YOUR FRONT DOOR.

• •

Company President: We had three outstanding applicants for the vice president position. However, in my opinion Mr. Morgan is most deserving of promotion, so he will be our new vice president. Is there anything you'd like to say, Mr. Morgan?

Mr. Morgan: Yes, sir! Thanks a lot, Dad.

• •

What kind of education do you need to work as a store greeter? Just a "Hi" school diploma.

Hi!

Jimmy: I used to be a racecar driver. Now I'm unemployed.
Zimmy: What happened?
Jimmy: There was a stock car market crash.

• •

Boss: Why are you late for work, Mr. Broom?
Mr. Broom: I overswept.

• •

Joe: Yesterday I went to apply for a job and fell face first in wet cement.
Moe: Well at least you made a good impression.

• •

Zack: I have a great job.
Mack: What do you do?
Zack: I'm the team dentist for a pro hockey team.

• •

KOOKY QUESTION:
Do plumbers have pipe dreams?

Sal: I used to work in the circus as a trapeze artist.

Al: What happened?
Sal: I was let go.

WHAT DID THE SICK SHOE SAY TO THE COBBLER?

PLEASE HEEL ME.

Knock! Knock!
Who's there?
Yule.
Yule who?
Yule be glad you hired me.

What did the sailor say at his wedding ceremony?
Aye Aye Do.

Then there was the owner of a dry-cleaning store who held a press conference to announce his grand opening.

~~~~~~~~~~~~~~~~~~~~~~~~

Man: *I'd like to work in men's clothing.*
Personal director: **Well, I have a job that may suit you.**

Not fun

CHAPTER
**** 10 ****
Daffy Definitions

DIETING – the victory of mind over platter.

DIVINE – what de grapes grow on.

FLOOD – a river too big for its bridges.

* *

BOW – a fiddlestick.

BARBED WIRE – a sarcastic telegram.

* * * * * * * * * * * * * *

DUST – mud with the juice squeezed out.

EGG – a bird's hometown.

STEAM – hot water that's blowing its top.

SKIING – A fall sport.

• •

SHEPHERD – a person all kids flock to.

EGOTIST – someone who's always me-deep in conversation.

FLASHLIGHT – a case used to carry dead batteries.

• •

GRAND CANYON – the hole of fame.

ENLISTMENT PAPERS – a service contract.

HOG WASH – a pig's laundry.

• •

IDEAL – my turn to shuffle the cards.

PARADOX – a mallard and his mate.

LAUGH – a smile that can't contain its enthusiasm.

TENSION – what the sergeant shouts to his soldiers.

SAUNA BATH – a safe way of getting into hot water.

BREAD – raw toast.

BRAGGART – a person who opens his mouth and puts his foot in it.

BOYCOTT – a small bed for a male child.

GOOSE PIMPLES
– duck acne.

LAWSUIT -- A
POLICEMAN'S UNIFORM.

CLOUD BANK–
a place to save
your money for a rainy day.

MINE OWNERS -- COAL-HEARTED PEOPLE.

MIDDLE AGES – knight time.

SNORING -- SHEET MUSIC.

SAUNA BATH – a slimming pool.

SKI JUMP -- A SOAR SPOT.

UNIVERSITY – a mental
institution.

ACTRESS -- A PERSON WHO WORKS HARD AT NOT BEING HERSELF.

ANTARCTIC – snowman's land.

• •

BEE -- A BUZZY BUSYBODY.

ILLEGAL – a sick bird of prey.

• •

FLOWER SHOP -- A BUDDING BUSINESS.

FENCING MASTER – a person with a duel personality.

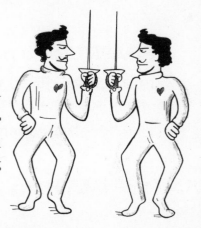

• •

MEDITATION -- AN INNER CALM SYSTEM.

PETRIFIED FOREST - a bunch of trees that came up the hard way.

THIEF -- a person who has a habit of finding things before others lose them.

****

SECRET - something we tell everyone not to tell anyone else.

BACTERIA -- the cafeteria's rear annex.

BOASTER - a person with whom it is sooner done than said.

****

BARBER SHOP -- a hairport.

LEOPARD - a dotted lion.

MISS AMERICA CONTEST -- the lass roundup.

****

FEMALE WRESTLER - the belle of the brawl.

RIDING -- the art of keeping a horse between you and the ground.

• •

TEARS -
remorse code.

TENNIS PRO -- a network executive.

* * * * * * * * * *

SURGEON - the person who was a cut-up at medical school.

• •

FIGHT ARENA - a punch bowl.

HYPOCHONDRIAC -- a person with plenty of sham pain.

* *

KLEPTOMANIAC - a person who helps herself because she can't help herself.

GOSSIP – a person with a real sense of rumor.

NAPKIN – *a cloth laptop.*

. . . .

ABSTRACT ARTIST – a person who draws his or her own confusions.

PEACE – *the shortest distance between two wars.*

. . . .

TEMPER TANTRUM – call of the riled.

SEAMSTRESS – *a material girl.*

. . . .

WITCHES – hexperts.

VAMPIRE – *hemogoblin.*

FUMIGATION – a smoke-flea environment.

• • • • • • • • • • • • • • • • • • • •

COMPUTER GOSSIP – *chat rumors.*

PSYCHIATRIST – a person who doesn't have to worry as long as other people do.

• • • • • • • • • • • • • • • • • • • •

WAITRESS – *a woman who thinks money grows on trays.*

FLU SHOT – an ouch of prevention.

• • • • • • • • • • • • • • • • • • • •

SLOW POKE – *the kind of punch a tired boxer throws.*

GRAVY- a liquid magically attracted to ties.

SOCKS – gloves for your feet.

ROTISSERIE- a Ferris wheel for food.

CHAPTER **11**

Last Laughs

Why did the cow go to court?
She was involved in a dairy case.

Where did the farm girls have cheerleading practice?
In the root cellar.

CHESTER: SEE THAT GUY. HE'S FROM TURKEY.

LESTER: WHAT'S HIS NAME?

CHESTER: I DON'T KNOW, BUT HIS FEZ IS FAMILIAR.

Billy: A fly ball hit my baseball cap in the game today and I didn't even feel it.

Father: Why not?

Billy: I loaned my cap to Tommy.

Dude: What do you use that rope for?

Cowboy: I use it to catch cattle.

Dude: What do you use for bait?

Why shouldn't you lose your temper?
Because no one else wants it.

Who is the smartest pig in the world?
Albert Einsty.

What do you get when you tell bird jokes?
Cheep laughs.

Cowboy: I broke three wild horses this morning.
Dude: The next time you go riding, be more careful.

Show me an Australian wearing jockey shorts ... and I'll show you down underwear.

Lenny: *My mother gave me five dollars for being good today.*
Jenny: *Humph! And all this time I've been being good for nothing.*

Knock! Knock!
Who's there?
I bid.
I bid who?
I bid you farewell.

What famous painting did Leonardo Da Skeleton paint? The Bony Lisa.

What are the most fragile things in the world?
Promises. People almost always break them.

WHY DID THE CHIMP BUY JOGGING SHOES?

IT WANTED TO JOIN THE HUMAN RACE.

What do you get if you cross a hen and a hand?
Chicken fingers.

KNOCK! KNOCK!
WHO'S THERE?
WIRE.
WIRE WHO?
WIRE YOU BEING SO STUBBORN?

Little Melanie came home from her first day of school and scowled at her mother. "I'm never going back there!" she grunted. "Why not?" asked her puzzled mom.
"I can't read. I can't write. And the teacher won't let me talk! So what's the use?"

Molly: Do you want to hear a funny story about a giraffe's neck?
Dolly: That depends. How long is it?

Kate: My sister married a nice Irish boy.
Mary: Oh really?
Kate: No. O'Reilly.

Why can you trust an Invisible Man dressed in a business suit?
Because he has nothing up his sleeve.

Teacher: Name four animals that belong to the cat family.
Boy: Mother Cat, Father Cat, and two baby kittens.

• •

SIGN ON A CHICKEN COOP:

EMPLOYEES MUST WASH THEIR HENS.

What do you get if you cross a judge's chambers and a sea vessel?
A courtship.

Knock! Knock!
Who's there?
Roland.
Roland who?
Roland down a hill is fun.

Bill: What do you get if you cross a dinosaur and a skunk?
Will: I don't know, but you can smell it coming from miles away.

****

Who writes fairytales about poker games?

Mother Deuce.

• •

WHY DID THE GIRAFFE GO TO THE SKIN DOCTOR?

IT HAD A MOLE ON ITS NECK.

****

Why did the skin doctor tell the giraffe not to worry?
The mole on its neck was really a gopher.

What do you get if you cross your mouth and a whip?

A tongue lashing.

• •

What book about crows did Jack London write?

The Caw of the Wild.

• •

Why did Charles Dickens chicken cross the road?

To get to the author's side.

• •

How do you get a tired shepherd to relax? Give him a sheeping pill.

What do you get if you cross a boxer and a suitcase?
A punching bag.

WHAT DID THE PIMPLE SAY TO THE ZIT?

IT'S TIME FOR US TO BREAK OUT.

What happens if an inchworm is afraid of heights?
He just can't measure up.

Knock! Knock!
Who's there?
Oliver.
Oliver who?
Oliver relatives are unfriendly, too.

Knock! Knock!
Who's there?
Polk
Polk who?
Polk her in the eye if she looks through the peephole.

Father: *Why do you get such bad grades in school?*
Son: *I can't think of any answer.*
Father: *That explains it.*

• • • • • • • • • • • • • • • • • • • •

Mrs. Turtle: The zoo has a lot of visitors today. Don't you want to see them?
Mr. Turtle: No. I'm through sticking my neck out for people.

• • • • • • • • • • • • • • • • • • • •

What do you call a well-behaved boa constrictor? A civil serpent.

AFTER YOU!

• • • • • • • • • • • • • • • • • • • •

How do you deal with a spoiled kid who wants ice cream?
Good humor him.

Which bone tells a lot of jokes?
The humorous.

****

Knock! Knock!
Who's there?
Wayne.
Wayne who?
Wayne is good for the front lawn.

What did one
shepherd say to the other
when the wolf pack attacked?

Don't give up the sheep.

Knock! Knock!
Who's there?
Kit.
Kit who?
Kit out of my way. I'm coming through.

UNCLE AL: I DON'T MIND RUNNING INTO
DEBT. IT'S RUNNING INTO CREDITORS
THAT EMBARRASSES ME.

Uncle: Did the Devil make you kick the neighbor's boy in the seat of the pants?
Nephew: Yes, uncle. But punching him in the nose was my own idea.

DAFFY DEFINITIONS:

Medicine Ball –
a gala dance for sick people.

Waiter – a person who believes money grows on trays.

Punter – A gridiron
athlete who foots his bill.

**Palm Tree – A handy
plant to have around.**

Spider – a hairy yoyo
with legs that
catches bugs.

WHAT DO YOU GET IF YOU CROSS A TURTLE AND AN ATM? A MACHINE THAT SHELLS OUT CASH.

What do you call insects that live in an ant farm?

Tenants.

Dina: I heard that all of King Arthur's soldiers suffered from insomnia.

Gina: Wow! Now that's a lot of sleepless knights.

SIGN ON A PLUMBER'S SHOP:

Repair your sink or swim.

Why did the little light bulb skip a grade? He was bright.

Tina: My boyfriend gave me a handful of pearls.
Gina: Why didn't he give you a pearl necklace?
Tina: I don't take gifts if they have strings attached to them.

A traveler staying in a cheap hotel room called the desk clerk to complain. "There's a mouse on my bed," the man grumbled. "What are you going to do about it?" "Relax," instructed the desk clerk. "The snake that lives under your bed will snap him up."

Artie: Did you hear the joke about the drought?
Marty: Is it dry humor?

Boss: Why are you asking for a raise?
Employee: Because somehow my family found out other people eat three times a day.

· ·

BENNY: I PAID FIFTY CENTS APIECE FOR THESE NEW JOKES.
LENNY: I'M SURE YOU'LL GET SOME CHEAP LAUGHS.

· ·

What do you get if you cross a band member and a cheerleader?

Musical cheers.

· ·

Why did the fish jump out of the lake and into the air during a rainstorm? He was tired of baths and wanted to take a shower.

Knock! Knock!
Who's there?
I'm Shad.
I'm Shad who?
I'm Shad to see you go.

● ● ● ● ● ● ● ● ● ● ● ● ● ● ● ● ● ● ●

ATTENTION: The cost of repairing this washing machine is spinning out of control.

● ● ● ● ● ● ● ● ● ● ● ● ● ● ● ● ● ● ●

Teenage girl: Mom, the girl next door has a prom dress just like mine.
Mother: I guess that means you want another prom dress.
Teenage girl: Well it would be easier than moving to a new school district.

● ● ● ● ● ● ● ● ● ● ● ● ● ● ● ● ● ● ● ●

Why did Bambi join the Air Force during World War II?
He wanted to be a bombadeer.

How much did the psychiatrist charge his elephant patient?

Two hundred dollars for the visit and eight hundred dollars for the broken couch.

* * * * * * * * * * * * *

ATTENTION: Financial success is relative. The more financial success, the more relatives.

* * * * * * * * * * * * *

Wife: How'd you do in the marathon today?

Husband: Fine. I would have finished first if two hundred runners didn't finish ahead of me.

KEN: WHERE DID YOU GET THOSE BIG BLUE EYES?

JEN: THEY CAME WITH MY FACE.

Dork: What's today's date?
Mork: Check the newspaper in your back pocket. The paper has the date on it.
Dork: That's no help. It's yesterday's paper.

Lady: I want a skirt to wear around the house.
Salesgirl: What size skirt does your house wear, ma'am?

* * * * * * * * * * *

What do you get if you cross a rude kid and a watch?
A clock that tocks back.

* * * * * * * * * * * * * *

Knock! Knock!
Who's there?
Kennedy.
Kennedy who?
Kennedy in math keep you out of college?